50 Cozy Winter Kitchen Dinner Recipes

By: Kelly Johnson

Table of Contents

- Classic Beef Stew
- Chicken and Dumplings
- Creamy Tomato Basil Soup
- Baked Ziti with Sausage
- Butternut Squash Risotto
- Slow Cooker Chili
- Beef and Barley Soup
- Chicken Pot Pie
- Moroccan Lamb Tagine
- Loaded Baked Potato Soup
- Stuffed Bell Peppers
- Mushroom Stroganoff
- Pasta e Fagioli
- Cozy Chicken Noodle Soup
- Shepherd's Pie
- Spaghetti and Meatballs
- Creamy Tuscan Chicken
- Sloppy Joes with Sweet Potato Fries
- Balsamic Glazed Roasted Chicken
- Vegetable Curry with Rice
- Pork Chops with Apples and Onions
- Shrimp and Grits
- Slow-Cooked Beef and Vegetable Soup
- Chicken Alfredo Bake
- Cabbage Roll Casserole
- Eggplant Parmesan
- Goulash
- Beef Enchiladas
- Pumpkin and Sage Pasta
- Cornbread Topped Chili
- Creamy Mushroom Chicken
- Spinach and Ricotta Stuffed Shells
- Teriyaki Chicken Stir-Fry
- Ratatouille
- Savory Quinoa and Vegetable Bake
- Chicken and Wild Rice Casserole

- Grilled Cheese and Tomato Soup
- Spiced Lentil and Carrot Stew
- Jambalaya
- Beef Tacos with Warm Corn Tortillas
- Thai Green Curry
- Italian Sausage and Peppers
- Ramen with Pork Belly
- Shrimp Chowder
- Vegetable Lasagna
- Chicken and Mushroom Risotto
- Sweet Potato and Black Bean Tacos
- Honey Garlic Glazed Salmon
- Quinoa and Roasted Vegetable Bowl
- Braised Short Ribs

Classic Beef Stew

Ingredients

- 2 lbs beef chuck, cut into 1-inch cubes
- 1/4 cup all-purpose flour
- 2 tablespoons olive oil
- 1 onion, chopped
- 3 cloves garlic, minced
- 4 cups beef broth
- 3 carrots, sliced
- 3 potatoes, diced
- 2 tablespoons tomato paste
- 1 teaspoon dried thyme
- Salt and pepper to taste

Instructions

1. **Brown the Beef:** In a large pot, toss the beef cubes in flour. Heat olive oil over medium-high heat and brown the beef in batches. Remove and set aside.
2. **Sauté Aromatics:** In the same pot, add onion and garlic, cooking until soft.
3. **Combine Ingredients:** Return beef to the pot, add broth, carrots, potatoes, tomato paste, thyme, salt, and pepper.
4. **Simmer:** Bring to a boil, then reduce heat and simmer for about 1.5 to 2 hours, until the beef is tender.

Chicken and Dumplings

Ingredients

- 1 lb chicken breast, diced
- 4 cups chicken broth
- 2 cups mixed vegetables (carrots, peas, corn)
- 1 onion, chopped
- 1 teaspoon dried thyme
- 1 cup all-purpose flour
- 1 tablespoon baking powder
- 1/2 cup milk
- 1/4 cup butter, melted
- Salt and pepper to taste

Instructions

1. **Cook Chicken:** In a large pot, bring chicken broth to a simmer. Add chicken, vegetables, onion, thyme, salt, and pepper.
2. **Make Dumplings:** In a bowl, combine flour, baking powder, milk, and melted butter. Stir until just combined.
3. **Add Dumplings:** Drop spoonfuls of the dough into the simmering broth. Cover and cook for about 15 minutes until the dumplings are cooked through.

Creamy Tomato Basil Soup

Ingredients

- 2 cans (14.5 oz each) diced tomatoes
- 1 cup chicken or vegetable broth
- 1 onion, chopped
- 3 cloves garlic, minced
- 1 cup heavy cream
- 1/4 cup fresh basil, chopped
- Salt and pepper to taste
- 1 tablespoon olive oil

Instructions

1. **Sauté Aromatics:** In a pot, heat olive oil over medium heat. Add onion and garlic, cooking until soft.
2. **Add Tomatoes and Broth:** Stir in diced tomatoes and broth. Simmer for about 15 minutes.
3. **Blend and Cream:** Use an immersion blender to puree the soup. Stir in cream and basil, and season with salt and pepper.

Baked Ziti with Sausage

Ingredients

- 1 lb ziti pasta
- 1 lb Italian sausage, casing removed
- 4 cups marinara sauce
- 2 cups ricotta cheese
- 2 cups shredded mozzarella cheese
- 1/2 cup grated Parmesan cheese
- 1 teaspoon Italian seasoning
- Salt and pepper to taste

Instructions

1. **Cook Pasta:** Preheat oven to 375°F (190°C). Cook ziti according to package instructions. Drain and set aside.
2. **Brown Sausage:** In a skillet, cook sausage until browned.
3. **Mix Ingredients:** In a large bowl, combine cooked ziti, sausage, marinara sauce, ricotta, half the mozzarella, Italian seasoning, salt, and pepper.
4. **Bake:** Transfer to a baking dish, top with remaining mozzarella and Parmesan. Bake for 25-30 minutes until bubbly.

Butternut Squash Risotto

Ingredients

- 1 medium butternut squash, peeled and cubed
- 1 cup Arborio rice
- 4 cups chicken or vegetable broth
- 1 onion, chopped
- 2 cloves garlic, minced
- 1/2 cup white wine (optional)
- 1/2 cup grated Parmesan cheese
- 2 tablespoons olive oil
- Salt and pepper to taste

Instructions

1. **Roast Squash:** Preheat oven to 400°F (200°C). Toss squash with olive oil, salt, and pepper. Roast for 25-30 minutes until tender.
2. **Sauté Aromatics:** In a pot, heat olive oil over medium heat. Add onion and garlic, cooking until soft.
3. **Cook Risotto:** Add Arborio rice, stirring for 1-2 minutes. Gradually add broth, one ladle at a time, stirring constantly until absorbed.
4. **Finish Risotto:** Stir in roasted squash and Parmesan cheese, and season to taste.

Slow Cooker Chili

Ingredients

- 1 lb ground beef or turkey
- 1 can (15 oz) kidney beans, drained
- 1 can (15 oz) black beans, drained
- 1 can (28 oz) crushed tomatoes
- 1 onion, chopped
- 1 bell pepper, chopped
- 2 tablespoons chili powder
- 1 teaspoon cumin
- Salt and pepper to taste

Instructions

1. **Brown Meat:** In a skillet, brown the ground meat. Transfer to the slow cooker.
2. **Combine Ingredients:** Add beans, crushed tomatoes, onion, bell pepper, chili powder, cumin, salt, and pepper to the slow cooker.
3. **Cook:** Set the slow cooker on low for 6-8 hours or high for 3-4 hours.

Beef and Barley Soup

Ingredients

- 1 lb beef stew meat, cubed
- 1/4 cup barley
- 1 onion, chopped
- 3 carrots, sliced
- 3 celery stalks, chopped
- 4 cups beef broth
- 2 tablespoons tomato paste
- 1 teaspoon dried thyme
- Salt and pepper to taste

Instructions

1. **Brown Beef:** In a pot, brown the beef cubes over medium heat.
2. **Add Vegetables:** Add onion, carrots, and celery. Cook for a few minutes until softened.
3. **Combine Ingredients:** Stir in broth, barley, tomato paste, thyme, salt, and pepper.
4. **Simmer:** Bring to a boil, then reduce heat and simmer for 1.5 hours until beef is tender.

Chicken Pot Pie

Ingredients

- 2 cups cooked chicken, shredded
- 1 cup mixed vegetables (peas, carrots, corn)
- 1/4 cup butter
- 1/4 cup all-purpose flour
- 2 cups chicken broth
- 1 cup milk
- 1 teaspoon dried thyme
- 1 pre-made pie crust

Instructions

1. **Make Filling:** In a pot, melt butter over medium heat. Stir in flour, cooking for 1-2 minutes. Gradually add chicken broth and milk, stirring until thickened.
2. **Combine Ingredients:** Add shredded chicken, mixed vegetables, thyme, salt, and pepper.
3. **Assemble Pie:** Pour filling into a pie dish and top with pie crust. Cut slits for steam to escape.
4. **Bake:** Preheat oven to 425°F (220°C) and bake for 30-35 minutes until golden brown.

Moroccan Lamb Tagine

Ingredients

- 2 lbs lamb shoulder, cut into cubes
- 1 onion, chopped
- 3 cloves garlic, minced
- 2 teaspoons ground cumin
- 1 teaspoon ground cinnamon
- 1 teaspoon ground ginger
- 1 can (14 oz) diced tomatoes
- 1 cup chicken or beef broth
- 1 cup dried apricots, chopped
- 1 can (15 oz) chickpeas, drained
- 2 tablespoons olive oil
- Salt and pepper to taste
- Fresh cilantro for garnish

Instructions

1. **Sauté Aromatics:** In a large pot or tagine, heat olive oil over medium heat. Add onion and garlic, cooking until soft.
2. **Brown Lamb:** Add lamb cubes, cumin, cinnamon, ginger, salt, and pepper. Brown the lamb on all sides.
3. **Combine Ingredients:** Stir in diced tomatoes, broth, and apricots. Bring to a boil, then reduce heat and simmer for about 1.5 hours.
4. **Add Chickpeas:** Stir in chickpeas and simmer for an additional 20 minutes. Garnish with cilantro before serving.

Loaded Baked Potato Soup

Ingredients

- 4 large potatoes, peeled and diced
- 1 onion, chopped
- 3 cloves garlic, minced
- 4 cups chicken or vegetable broth
- 1 cup heavy cream
- 1 cup shredded cheddar cheese
- 1/2 cup sour cream
- 1/4 cup green onions, chopped
- Salt and pepper to taste
- 4 slices bacon, cooked and crumbled (optional)

Instructions

1. **Cook Potatoes:** In a large pot, combine potatoes, onion, garlic, and broth. Bring to a boil and simmer until potatoes are tender.
2. **Blend Soup:** Use an immersion blender to puree the soup to your desired consistency.
3. **Add Cream and Cheese:** Stir in heavy cream, cheddar cheese, sour cream, salt, and pepper. Heat until warmed through.
4. **Serve:** Top with green onions and crumbled bacon if desired.

Stuffed Bell Peppers

Ingredients

- 4 large bell peppers, tops removed and seeds discarded
- 1 lb ground beef or turkey
- 1 cup cooked rice
- 1 can (14 oz) diced tomatoes
- 1 onion, chopped
- 2 cloves garlic, minced
- 1 teaspoon Italian seasoning
- Salt and pepper to taste
- 1 cup shredded mozzarella cheese

Instructions

1. **Preheat Oven:** Preheat oven to 375°F (190°C).
2. **Cook Filling:** In a skillet, brown the ground meat with onion and garlic. Drain excess fat.
3. **Mix Ingredients:** Stir in cooked rice, diced tomatoes, Italian seasoning, salt, and pepper.
4. **Stuff Peppers:** Fill each bell pepper with the meat mixture and place in a baking dish. Top with mozzarella cheese.
5. **Bake:** Cover with foil and bake for 30 minutes. Remove foil and bake for an additional 15 minutes until cheese is melted.

Mushroom Stroganoff

Ingredients

- 8 oz mushrooms, sliced
- 1 onion, chopped
- 2 cloves garlic, minced
- 1 cup vegetable broth
- 1 cup sour cream
- 2 tablespoons flour
- 1 tablespoon soy sauce
- 1 teaspoon paprika
- 2 tablespoons olive oil
- Salt and pepper to taste
- Cooked egg noodles for serving

Instructions

1. **Sauté Vegetables:** In a skillet, heat olive oil over medium heat. Add onions and garlic, cooking until soft.
2. **Cook Mushrooms:** Add mushrooms and cook until browned.
3. **Make Sauce:** Sprinkle flour over the mushrooms and stir. Gradually add vegetable broth, soy sauce, and paprika. Bring to a simmer.
4. **Finish Sauce:** Stir in sour cream, salt, and pepper. Serve over cooked egg noodles.

Pasta e Fagioli

Ingredients

- 1 cup ditalini pasta
- 1 can (15 oz) cannellini beans, drained
- 1 can (14 oz) diced tomatoes
- 4 cups vegetable broth
- 1 onion, chopped
- 2 cloves garlic, minced
- 2 carrots, diced
- 1 teaspoon Italian seasoning
- Salt and pepper to taste

Instructions

1. **Sauté Vegetables:** In a large pot, heat olive oil and sauté onion, garlic, and carrots until soft.
2. **Add Broth and Beans:** Stir in broth, diced tomatoes, cannellini beans, Italian seasoning, salt, and pepper. Bring to a boil.
3. **Cook Pasta:** Add pasta and simmer until al dente.
4. **Serve:** Adjust seasoning and serve hot.

Cozy Chicken Noodle Soup

Ingredients

- 2 cups cooked chicken, shredded
- 4 cups chicken broth
- 2 cups egg noodles
- 1 onion, chopped
- 3 carrots, sliced
- 3 celery stalks, chopped
- 2 cloves garlic, minced
- 1 teaspoon dried thyme
- Salt and pepper to taste

Instructions

1. **Cook Vegetables:** In a large pot, sauté onion, carrots, and celery until soft. Add garlic and cook for 1 minute.
2. **Add Broth:** Pour in chicken broth and bring to a boil.
3. **Add Chicken and Noodles:** Stir in shredded chicken, egg noodles, thyme, salt, and pepper. Simmer until noodles are tender.

Shepherd's Pie

Ingredients

- 1 lb ground lamb or beef
- 1 onion, chopped
- 2 carrots, diced
- 1 cup frozen peas
- 2 tablespoons tomato paste
- 1 cup beef broth
- 2 lbs potatoes, peeled and cubed
- 1/2 cup milk
- 1/4 cup butter
- Salt and pepper to taste

Instructions

1. **Cook Meat and Vegetables:** In a skillet, brown ground meat with onion and carrots. Stir in tomato paste and broth. Add peas and simmer.
2. **Make Mashed Potatoes:** Boil potatoes until tender, then mash with milk, butter, salt, and pepper.
3. **Assemble Pie:** Spread meat mixture in a baking dish, top with mashed potatoes.
4. **Bake:** Preheat oven to 400°F (200°C) and bake for 20-25 minutes until golden.

Spaghetti and Meatballs

Ingredients

- 1 lb ground beef
- 1/2 cup breadcrumbs
- 1/4 cup grated Parmesan cheese
- 1 egg
- 2 cups marinara sauce
- 1 lb spaghetti
- Salt and pepper to taste

Instructions

1. **Make Meatballs:** In a bowl, combine ground beef, breadcrumbs, Parmesan, egg, salt, and pepper. Form into meatballs.
2. **Cook Meatballs:** In a skillet, brown meatballs on all sides.
3. **Add Sauce:** Pour marinara sauce over meatballs and simmer for 20 minutes.
4. **Cook Pasta:** Cook spaghetti according to package instructions. Serve meatballs over spaghetti.

Creamy Tuscan Chicken

Ingredients

- 4 chicken breasts
- 2 cups spinach
- 1 cup cherry tomatoes, halved
- 1 cup heavy cream
- 1/2 cup grated Parmesan cheese
- 2 cloves garlic, minced
- 2 tablespoons olive oil
- Salt and pepper to taste

Instructions

1. **Cook Chicken:** In a skillet, heat olive oil over medium heat. Season chicken with salt and pepper, and cook until golden and cooked through. Remove and set aside.
2. **Sauté Spinach and Tomatoes:** In the same skillet, add garlic, spinach, and tomatoes, cooking until spinach wilts.
3. **Make Sauce:** Stir in heavy cream and Parmesan, bringing to a simmer.
4. **Combine:** Return chicken to the skillet and coat with the sauce. Serve hot.

Sloppy Joes with Sweet Potato Fries

Ingredients

- **For Sloppy Joes:**
    - 1 lb ground beef or turkey
    - 1 onion, chopped
    - 1 green bell pepper, chopped
    - 1 cup ketchup
    - 2 tablespoons brown sugar
    - 1 tablespoon Worcestershire sauce
    - 1 teaspoon garlic powder
    - Salt and pepper to taste
    - 4 hamburger buns
- **For Sweet Potato Fries:**
    - 2 large sweet potatoes, cut into fries
    - 2 tablespoons olive oil
    - 1 teaspoon paprika
    - Salt and pepper to taste

Instructions

1. **Prepare Sweet Potato Fries:** Preheat oven to 425°F (220°C). Toss sweet potato fries with olive oil, paprika, salt, and pepper. Spread on a baking sheet and bake for 25-30 minutes until crispy.
2. **Cook Sloppy Joes:** In a skillet, brown the ground meat with onion and bell pepper. Drain excess fat. Stir in ketchup, brown sugar, Worcestershire sauce, garlic powder, salt, and pepper. Simmer for 10 minutes.
3. **Serve:** Spoon the meat mixture onto hamburger buns and serve with sweet potato fries.

Balsamic Glazed Roasted Chicken

Ingredients

- 4 chicken thighs, bone-in and skin-on
- 1/4 cup balsamic vinegar
- 2 tablespoons honey
- 2 cloves garlic, minced
- 1 tablespoon olive oil
- Salt and pepper to taste
- Fresh rosemary for garnish

Instructions

1. **Preheat Oven:** Preheat oven to 400°F (200°C).
2. **Make Glaze:** In a bowl, whisk together balsamic vinegar, honey, garlic, olive oil, salt, and pepper.
3. **Prepare Chicken:** Place chicken thighs in a baking dish and pour the balsamic glaze over them.
4. **Roast Chicken:** Bake for 35-40 minutes until chicken is cooked through and has a nice glaze. Garnish with fresh rosemary before serving.

Vegetable Curry with Rice

Ingredients

- 1 cup mixed vegetables (carrots, peas, bell peppers)
- 1 onion, chopped
- 2 cloves garlic, minced
- 1 tablespoon curry powder
- 1 can (14 oz) coconut milk
- 1 cup vegetable broth
- 2 cups cooked rice
- Salt to taste
- Fresh cilantro for garnish

Instructions

1. **Sauté Onions:** In a pot, sauté onion and garlic until soft.
2. **Add Vegetables and Spices:** Stir in mixed vegetables and curry powder, cooking for 2-3 minutes.
3. **Add Liquids:** Pour in coconut milk and vegetable broth. Simmer for 15-20 minutes until vegetables are tender.
4. **Serve:** Season with salt and serve over cooked rice. Garnish with cilantro.

Pork Chops with Apples and Onions

Ingredients

- 4 pork chops
- 2 apples, sliced
- 1 onion, sliced
- 1 tablespoon olive oil
- 1 teaspoon cinnamon
- Salt and pepper to taste

Instructions

1. **Sear Pork Chops:** In a skillet, heat olive oil over medium-high heat. Season pork chops with salt and pepper and sear until browned on both sides. Remove from skillet.
2. **Cook Apples and Onions:** In the same skillet, add onions and apples. Sprinkle with cinnamon and cook until soft.
3. **Combine and Finish Cooking:** Return pork chops to the skillet, cover, and cook until pork is cooked through and apples are tender.

Shrimp and Grits

Ingredients

- 1 lb shrimp, peeled and deveined
- 1 cup grits
- 4 cups water or chicken broth
- 1 cup shredded cheddar cheese
- 4 slices bacon, cooked and crumbled
- 1/2 cup green onions, chopped
- 1 tablespoon butter
- Salt and pepper to taste

Instructions

1. **Cook Grits:** In a pot, bring water or broth to a boil. Stir in grits, reduce heat, and simmer until thickened. Stir in cheese, salt, and pepper.
2. **Cook Shrimp:** In a skillet, melt butter and cook shrimp until pink and cooked through. Stir in crumbled bacon and green onions.
3. **Serve:** Spoon grits into bowls and top with shrimp mixture.

Slow-Cooked Beef and Vegetable Soup

Ingredients

- 1 lb beef stew meat, cut into cubes
- 4 cups beef broth
- 2 carrots, diced
- 2 potatoes, diced
- 1 onion, chopped
- 2 cloves garlic, minced
- 1 teaspoon thyme
- Salt and pepper to taste

Instructions

1. **Combine Ingredients:** In a slow cooker, combine beef, broth, carrots, potatoes, onion, garlic, thyme, salt, and pepper.
2. **Cook Soup:** Cover and cook on low for 6-8 hours or until beef is tender.
3. **Serve:** Adjust seasoning if necessary and serve hot.

Chicken Alfredo Bake

Ingredients

- 2 cups cooked pasta (penne or rigatoni)
- 2 cups cooked chicken, shredded
- 2 cups Alfredo sauce
- 1 cup shredded mozzarella cheese
- 1/2 cup grated Parmesan cheese
- 1 teaspoon garlic powder
- Salt and pepper to taste

Instructions

1. **Preheat Oven:** Preheat oven to 375°F (190°C).
2. **Mix Ingredients:** In a large bowl, combine cooked pasta, chicken, Alfredo sauce, mozzarella, garlic powder, salt, and pepper.
3. **Bake:** Transfer mixture to a baking dish and top with Parmesan cheese. Bake for 20-25 minutes until bubbly and golden.

Cabbage Roll Casserole

Ingredients

- 1 lb ground beef
- 1 onion, chopped
- 1 head of cabbage, chopped
- 2 cups cooked rice
- 1 can (14 oz) diced tomatoes
- 1 can (8 oz) tomato sauce
- 2 tablespoons brown sugar
- Salt and pepper to taste

Instructions

1. **Cook Beef and Onion:** In a skillet, brown ground beef with onion. Drain excess fat.
2. **Combine Ingredients:** In a large bowl, mix cooked beef, cabbage, rice, diced tomatoes, tomato sauce, brown sugar, salt, and pepper.
3. **Bake Casserole:** Pour mixture into a baking dish and cover. Bake at 350°F (175°C) for 45 minutes until cabbage is tender.

Eggplant Parmesan

Ingredients

- 2 medium eggplants, sliced into 1/4-inch rounds
- 2 cups marinara sauce
- 2 cups shredded mozzarella cheese
- 1 cup grated Parmesan cheese
- 1 cup all-purpose flour
- 2 eggs, beaten
- 2 cups breadcrumbs
- Salt and pepper to taste
- Olive oil for frying

Instructions

1. **Preheat Oven:** Preheat oven to 375°F (190°C).
2. **Prepare Eggplant:** Sprinkle eggplant slices with salt and let them sit for 30 minutes to draw out moisture. Rinse and pat dry.
3. **Bread Eggplant:** Dredge each slice in flour, dip in beaten eggs, and coat with breadcrumbs.
4. **Fry Eggplant:** In a skillet, heat olive oil over medium heat. Fry eggplant slices until golden brown on both sides.
5. **Layer in Baking Dish:** In a baking dish, layer marinara sauce, eggplant, mozzarella, and Parmesan. Repeat layers, finishing with cheese on top.
6. **Bake:** Bake for 25-30 minutes until cheese is bubbly and golden.

Goulash

Ingredients

- 1 lb ground beef
- 1 onion, chopped
- 2 cloves garlic, minced
- 1 can (14 oz) diced tomatoes
- 2 cups elbow macaroni
- 2 cups beef broth
- 2 tablespoons paprika
- 1 teaspoon Italian seasoning
- Salt and pepper to taste

Instructions

1. **Cook Beef and Onions:** In a large pot, brown ground beef with onion and garlic. Drain excess fat.
2. **Add Ingredients:** Stir in diced tomatoes, macaroni, beef broth, paprika, Italian seasoning, salt, and pepper.
3. **Simmer:** Bring to a boil, then reduce heat and simmer for 15-20 minutes until pasta is tender.

Beef Enchiladas

Ingredients

- 1 lb ground beef
- 1 onion, chopped
- 1 can (10 oz) enchilada sauce
- 8 flour tortillas
- 2 cups shredded cheddar cheese
- 1 can (15 oz) black beans, rinsed and drained
- 1 teaspoon cumin
- Salt and pepper to taste

Instructions

1. **Preheat Oven:** Preheat oven to 350°F (175°C).
2. **Cook Beef:** In a skillet, brown ground beef with onion. Stir in cumin, salt, and pepper.
3. **Assemble Enchiladas:** Spread a little enchilada sauce in the bottom of a baking dish. Fill each tortilla with beef, black beans, and cheese. Roll up and place seam side down in the dish.
4. **Top with Sauce and Cheese:** Pour remaining enchilada sauce over the top and sprinkle with more cheese.
5. **Bake:** Bake for 20-25 minutes until cheese is melted and bubbly.

Pumpkin and Sage Pasta

Ingredients

- 8 oz pasta (fettuccine or your choice)
- 1 can (15 oz) pumpkin puree
- 1/2 cup heavy cream
- 1/4 cup grated Parmesan cheese
- 2 tablespoons fresh sage, chopped
- Salt and pepper to taste
- Olive oil for cooking

Instructions

1. **Cook Pasta:** Cook pasta according to package instructions; drain.
2. **Make Sauce:** In a skillet, heat olive oil and sauté sage until fragrant. Add pumpkin puree and cream, stirring to combine.
3. **Combine:** Stir in cooked pasta and Parmesan cheese. Season with salt and pepper to taste.

Cornbread Topped Chili

Ingredients

- 1 lb ground beef
- 1 can (15 oz) kidney beans, drained
- 1 can (15 oz) black beans, drained
- 1 can (14 oz) diced tomatoes
- 1 can (8 oz) tomato sauce
- 1 onion, chopped
- 2 tablespoons chili powder
- 1 box cornbread mix

Instructions

1. **Cook Chili:** In a large pot, brown ground beef with onion. Stir in beans, tomatoes, tomato sauce, and chili powder. Simmer for 20-30 minutes.
2. **Prepare Cornbread:** Prepare cornbread mix according to package instructions.
3. **Assemble and Bake:** Pour chili into a baking dish, top with cornbread batter, and bake at 400°F (200°C) for 20-25 minutes until cornbread is golden.

Creamy Mushroom Chicken

Ingredients

- 4 chicken breasts
- 8 oz mushrooms, sliced
- 1 cup heavy cream
- 2 cloves garlic, minced
- 1 teaspoon thyme
- Salt and pepper to taste
- Olive oil for cooking

Instructions

1. **Cook Chicken:** In a skillet, heat olive oil over medium heat. Season chicken breasts with salt and pepper, and cook until golden brown and cooked through. Remove from skillet.
2. **Cook Mushrooms:** In the same skillet, add mushrooms and garlic. Sauté until mushrooms are tender.
3. **Make Sauce:** Stir in heavy cream and thyme. Bring to a simmer, then return chicken to the skillet and cook until heated through.

Spinach and Ricotta Stuffed Shells

Ingredients

- 12 jumbo pasta shells
- 1 cup ricotta cheese
- 2 cups spinach, cooked and chopped
- 1 cup marinara sauce
- 1 cup shredded mozzarella cheese
- 1/2 cup grated Parmesan cheese
- Salt and pepper to taste

Instructions

1. **Preheat Oven:** Preheat oven to 375°F (190°C).
2. **Cook Pasta:** Cook pasta shells according to package instructions; drain.
3. **Prepare Filling:** In a bowl, mix ricotta cheese, spinach, salt, and pepper. Stuff each shell with the mixture.
4. **Assemble:** Spread a layer of marinara sauce in a baking dish. Place stuffed shells on top and cover with remaining sauce. Sprinkle with mozzarella and Parmesan.
5. **Bake:** Bake for 25-30 minutes until cheese is melted and bubbly.

Teriyaki Chicken Stir-Fry

Ingredients

- 1 lb chicken breast, sliced
- 2 cups mixed vegetables (bell peppers, broccoli, carrots)
- 1/4 cup teriyaki sauce
- 2 tablespoons soy sauce
- 1 tablespoon sesame oil
- Cooked rice for serving

Instructions

1. **Cook Chicken:** In a skillet, heat sesame oil over medium heat. Add chicken and cook until browned and cooked through.
2. **Add Vegetables:** Stir in mixed vegetables and cook until tender-crisp.
3. **Add Sauce:** Pour teriyaki and soy sauce over the chicken and vegetables. Stir to combine and heat through.
4. **Serve:** Serve over cooked rice.

Ratatouille

Ingredients

- 1 eggplant, diced
- 1 zucchini, sliced
- 1 bell pepper, chopped
- 1 onion, chopped
- 2 cloves garlic, minced
- 4 ripe tomatoes, chopped
- 2 tablespoons olive oil
- 1 teaspoon dried basil
- 1 teaspoon dried thyme
- Salt and pepper to taste

Instructions

1. **Preheat Oven:** Preheat oven to 375°F (190°C).
2. **Sauté Vegetables:** In a large skillet, heat olive oil over medium heat. Add onion and garlic, cooking until soft.
3. **Add Remaining Vegetables:** Stir in eggplant, zucchini, and bell pepper, cooking for about 5 minutes.
4. **Add Tomatoes and Seasonings:** Add chopped tomatoes, basil, thyme, salt, and pepper. Stir to combine.
5. **Bake:** Transfer to a baking dish and bake for 30-35 minutes until vegetables are tender.

Savory Quinoa and Vegetable Bake

Ingredients

- 1 cup quinoa, rinsed
- 2 cups vegetable broth
- 1 cup mixed vegetables (carrots, peas, corn)
- 1/2 cup shredded cheese (cheddar or mozzarella)
- 2 eggs, beaten
- 1 teaspoon dried oregano
- Salt and pepper to taste

Instructions

1. **Preheat Oven:** Preheat oven to 350°F (175°C).
2. **Cook Quinoa:** In a saucepan, combine quinoa and vegetable broth. Bring to a boil, reduce heat, and simmer for 15 minutes.
3. **Mix Ingredients:** In a large bowl, combine cooked quinoa, mixed vegetables, cheese, eggs, oregano, salt, and pepper.
4. **Bake:** Pour mixture into a greased baking dish and bake for 25-30 minutes until set.

Chicken and Wild Rice Casserole

Ingredients

- 2 cups cooked wild rice
- 2 cups cooked chicken, shredded
- 1 cup cream of mushroom soup
- 1 cup chicken broth
- 1 cup frozen mixed vegetables
- 1 teaspoon garlic powder
- 1 teaspoon onion powder
- Salt and pepper to taste

Instructions

1. **Preheat Oven:** Preheat oven to 350°F (175°C).
2. **Combine Ingredients:** In a large bowl, combine wild rice, chicken, mushroom soup, chicken broth, mixed vegetables, garlic powder, onion powder, salt, and pepper.
3. **Transfer to Baking Dish:** Pour mixture into a greased casserole dish and spread evenly.
4. **Bake:** Bake for 30-35 minutes until heated through and bubbly.

Grilled Cheese and Tomato Soup

Ingredients

- 4 slices of bread
- 4 slices of cheese (cheddar or American)
- 2 tablespoons butter
- 1 can (14 oz) diced tomatoes
- 1 cup vegetable broth
- 1 teaspoon sugar
- 1 teaspoon dried basil
- Salt and pepper to taste

Instructions

1. **Make Tomato Soup:** In a saucepan, combine diced tomatoes, vegetable broth, sugar, basil, salt, and pepper. Simmer for 10-15 minutes.
2. **Prepare Grilled Cheese:** Heat a skillet over medium heat. Butter one side of each slice of bread, place cheese between two slices (buttered sides out), and cook until golden brown on both sides.
3. **Serve:** Serve grilled cheese with hot tomato soup for dipping.

Spiced Lentil and Carrot Stew

Ingredients

- 1 cup lentils, rinsed
- 2 carrots, diced
- 1 onion, chopped
- 2 cloves garlic, minced
- 1 teaspoon cumin
- 1 teaspoon coriander
- 4 cups vegetable broth
- Salt and pepper to taste

Instructions

1. **Sauté Vegetables:** In a large pot, heat olive oil over medium heat. Add onion and garlic, cooking until soft.
2. **Add Carrots and Spices:** Stir in diced carrots, cumin, and coriander, cooking for 2-3 minutes.
3. **Add Lentils and Broth:** Add lentils and vegetable broth. Bring to a boil, then reduce heat and simmer for 30-40 minutes until lentils are tender.
4. **Season:** Season with salt and pepper to taste.

Jambalaya

Ingredients

- 1 lb smoked sausage, sliced
- 1 lb shrimp, peeled and deveined
- 1 onion, chopped
- 1 bell pepper, chopped
- 2 cloves garlic, minced
- 1 can (14 oz) diced tomatoes
- 2 cups chicken broth
- 2 cups rice
- 2 teaspoons Cajun seasoning
- Salt and pepper to taste

Instructions

1. **Cook Sausage:** In a large pot, brown sausage over medium heat. Remove and set aside.
2. **Sauté Vegetables:** In the same pot, add onion, bell pepper, and garlic, cooking until soft.
3. **Combine Ingredients:** Stir in diced tomatoes, chicken broth, rice, Cajun seasoning, salt, and pepper. Bring to a boil.
4. **Simmer:** Reduce heat, cover, and simmer for 20 minutes. Add shrimp and sausage, cooking for an additional 5-10 minutes until shrimp are cooked through.

Beef Tacos with Warm Corn Tortillas

Ingredients

- 1 lb ground beef
- 1 taco seasoning packet
- 8 corn tortillas
- Toppings: shredded lettuce, diced tomatoes, cheese, salsa

Instructions

1. **Cook Beef:** In a skillet, brown ground beef over medium heat. Drain excess fat. Add taco seasoning and follow packet instructions.
2. **Warm Tortillas:** Heat corn tortillas in a skillet or microwave until warm.
3. **Assemble Tacos:** Fill each tortilla with beef and desired toppings.

Thai Green Curry

Ingredients

- 1 lb chicken, sliced
- 1 can (14 oz) coconut milk
- 2 tablespoons green curry paste
- 1 cup mixed vegetables (bell peppers, zucchini, eggplant)
- 2 tablespoons fish sauce
- Fresh basil for garnish

Instructions

1. **Cook Chicken:** In a skillet, cook chicken over medium heat until no longer pink.
2. **Add Curry Paste:** Stir in green curry paste and cook for 2-3 minutes.
3. **Add Coconut Milk and Vegetables:** Pour in coconut milk, add mixed vegetables, and fish sauce. Simmer for 10-15 minutes until vegetables are tender.
4. **Serve:** Garnish with fresh basil and serve with rice.

Italian Sausage and Peppers

Ingredients

- 1 lb Italian sausage (sweet or spicy)
- 2 bell peppers (red and green), sliced
- 1 onion, sliced
- 3 cloves garlic, minced
- 1 can (14 oz) diced tomatoes
- 2 tablespoons olive oil
- Salt and pepper to taste
- Fresh basil for garnish

Instructions

1. **Cook Sausage:** In a large skillet, heat olive oil over medium heat. Add sausage and cook until browned. Remove from skillet and set aside.
2. **Sauté Vegetables:** In the same skillet, add onion, garlic, and bell peppers. Sauté until softened.
3. **Combine Ingredients:** Add diced tomatoes and sausage back to the skillet. Season with salt and pepper, and simmer for 15 minutes.
4. **Serve:** Garnish with fresh basil and serve with crusty bread or over pasta.

Ramen with Pork Belly

Ingredients

- 4 cups chicken or pork broth
- 1 lb pork belly, sliced
- 2 packs of ramen noodles
- 2 soft-boiled eggs
- 1 cup bok choy, chopped
- 2 green onions, sliced
- 2 tablespoons soy sauce
- 1 tablespoon miso paste
- Sesame seeds for garnish

Instructions

1. **Cook Pork Belly:** In a skillet, cook pork belly over medium heat until crispy. Remove and set aside.
2. **Prepare Broth:** In a pot, combine broth, soy sauce, and miso paste. Bring to a simmer.
3. **Cook Ramen:** Add ramen noodles and bok choy to the broth, cooking according to package instructions.
4. **Serve:** Divide ramen into bowls, top with sliced pork belly, soft-boiled eggs, green onions, and sesame seeds.

Shrimp Chowder

Ingredients

- 1 lb shrimp, peeled and deveined
- 4 cups seafood or chicken broth
- 2 cups potatoes, diced
- 1 cup corn (fresh or frozen)
- 1 cup heavy cream
- 1 onion, chopped
- 2 cloves garlic, minced
- 2 tablespoons butter
- Salt and pepper to taste

Instructions

1. **Sauté Onion and Garlic:** In a large pot, melt butter over medium heat. Add onion and garlic, cooking until soft.
2. **Cook Potatoes:** Add diced potatoes and broth, bringing to a boil. Reduce heat and simmer until potatoes are tender.
3. **Add Shrimp and Corn:** Stir in shrimp and corn, cooking until shrimp are pink and cooked through.
4. **Add Cream:** Stir in heavy cream, season with salt and pepper, and heat through. Serve hot.

Vegetable Lasagna

Ingredients

- 9 lasagna noodles
- 2 cups ricotta cheese
- 2 cups mozzarella cheese, shredded
- 2 cups spinach, cooked
- 1 zucchini, sliced
- 1 bell pepper, diced
- 2 cups marinara sauce
- 1 teaspoon Italian seasoning
- Salt and pepper to taste

Instructions

1. **Preheat Oven:** Preheat oven to 375°F (190°C).
2. **Cook Noodles:** Cook lasagna noodles according to package instructions and drain.
3. **Layer Ingredients:** In a baking dish, spread a layer of marinara sauce, followed by noodles, ricotta, vegetables, mozzarella, and Italian seasoning. Repeat layers, finishing with noodles and sauce on top.
4. **Bake:** Cover with foil and bake for 25 minutes. Remove foil and bake for an additional 15 minutes until cheese is bubbly.

Chicken and Mushroom Risotto

Ingredients

- 1 cup Arborio rice
- 1 lb chicken breast, diced
- 4 cups chicken broth
- 1 cup mushrooms, sliced
- 1 onion, chopped
- 2 cloves garlic, minced
- 1/2 cup white wine (optional)
- 1/2 cup Parmesan cheese, grated
- 2 tablespoons butter
- Salt and pepper to taste

Instructions

1. **Cook Chicken:** In a skillet, heat butter over medium heat. Add chicken and cook until browned. Remove and set aside.
2. **Sauté Vegetables:** In the same skillet, add onion, garlic, and mushrooms, cooking until softened.
3. **Add Rice:** Stir in Arborio rice and cook for 1-2 minutes. If using, pour in white wine, stirring until absorbed.
4. **Add Broth:** Gradually add chicken broth, one ladle at a time, stirring until absorbed before adding more. Cook until rice is creamy and tender, about 18-20 minutes.
5. **Finish Risotto:** Stir in cooked chicken, Parmesan cheese, and season with salt and pepper. Serve hot.

Sweet Potato and Black Bean Tacos

Ingredients

- 2 medium sweet potatoes, peeled and diced
- 1 can black beans, drained and rinsed
- 1 teaspoon cumin
- 1 teaspoon chili powder
- Salt and pepper to taste
- 8 corn tortillas
- 1 avocado, sliced
- Fresh cilantro for garnish
- Lime wedges for serving

Instructions

1. **Cook Sweet Potatoes:** Preheat oven to 400°F (200°C). Toss diced sweet potatoes with olive oil, cumin, chili powder, salt, and pepper. Spread on a baking sheet and roast for 25-30 minutes until tender.
2. **Warm Tortillas:** In a skillet, lightly warm the corn tortillas until pliable.
3. **Assemble Tacos:** In each tortilla, add roasted sweet potatoes, black beans, and sliced avocado.
4. **Serve:** Garnish with fresh cilantro and serve with lime wedges.

Honey Garlic Glazed Salmon

Ingredients

- 4 salmon fillets
- 1/4 cup honey
- 2 tablespoons soy sauce
- 2 cloves garlic, minced
- 1 tablespoon olive oil
- Salt and pepper to taste
- Lemon wedges for serving

Instructions

1. **Prepare Marinade:** In a small bowl, whisk together honey, soy sauce, garlic, olive oil, salt, and pepper.
2. **Marinate Salmon:** Place salmon fillets in a shallow dish and pour the marinade over them. Let marinate for at least 15 minutes.
3. **Cook Salmon:** Preheat a skillet over medium heat. Remove salmon from marinade and cook for 4-5 minutes per side until cooked through and caramelized.
4. **Serve:** Serve with lemon wedges and drizzle any remaining glaze over the top.

Quinoa and Roasted Vegetable Bowl

Ingredients

- 1 cup quinoa, rinsed
- 2 cups vegetable broth or water
- 1 zucchini, diced
- 1 bell pepper, diced
- 1 red onion, chopped
- 2 tablespoons olive oil
- Salt and pepper to taste
- Fresh parsley for garnish

Instructions

1. **Cook Quinoa:** In a pot, combine quinoa and vegetable broth. Bring to a boil, then reduce heat and simmer for 15 minutes until quinoa is cooked and liquid is absorbed.
2. **Roast Vegetables:** Preheat oven to 425°F (220°C). Toss zucchini, bell pepper, and red onion with olive oil, salt, and pepper. Spread on a baking sheet and roast for 20-25 minutes until tender.
3. **Assemble Bowl:** In a bowl, combine cooked quinoa and roasted vegetables.
4. **Serve:** Garnish with fresh parsley and serve warm.

Braised Short Ribs

Ingredients

- 4 lbs beef short ribs
- 1 onion, chopped
- 2 carrots, chopped
- 2 celery stalks, chopped
- 4 cloves garlic, minced
- 2 cups red wine
- 2 cups beef broth
- 2 tablespoons tomato paste
- 2 sprigs fresh thyme
- Salt and pepper to taste

Instructions

1. **Sear Short Ribs:** In a large pot, heat oil over medium-high heat. Season short ribs with salt and pepper and sear until browned on all sides. Remove from pot and set aside.
2. **Sauté Vegetables:** In the same pot, add onion, carrots, celery, and garlic. Sauté until softened.
3. **Deglaze Pot:** Stir in red wine and scrape the bottom of the pot to release browned bits. Add beef broth, tomato paste, thyme, and short ribs back to the pot.
4. **Braise:** Bring to a simmer, cover, and reduce heat to low. Cook for 2.5 to 3 hours until ribs are tender.
5. **Serve:** Remove ribs from pot and serve with the sauce over mashed potatoes or polenta.

www.ingramcontent.com/pod-product-compliance
Lightning Source LLC
LaVergne TN
LVHW081334060526
838201LV00055B/2642